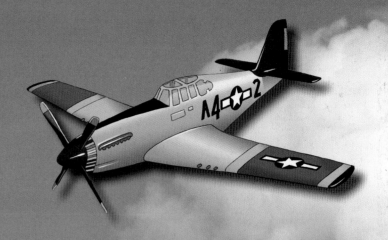

Tales of Famous HEROES

by Peter and Connie Roop   illustrated by Rebecca Zomchek

SCHOLASTIC REFERENCE
An imprint of
SCHOLASTIC

In honor of Susan Phelps Kaehler, M.D.

Susan, you have been my friend and heroine ever since you were the Troll and I was the Little Billy Goat Gruff. Because you followed your dream, women physicians can more easily follow their career paths.

With love,

Connie Betzer Roop

With thanks to Ed, who inspired this book.

For Gina, whose heroic editing efforts launched this book. Let's do more of the same.

Library of Congress Cataloging-in-Publication Data Available

ISBN 978-0-545-23750-5

10 9 8 7 6 5 4 3 2 1   10 11 12 13 14

Printed in Singapore   46

First printing, October 2010

Illustrations by Rebecca Zomchek

Contents

AMERICAN PATRIOTS

Paul Revere 1734–1818 and

Sybil Ludington 1761–1839

"Listen, my children, and you shall hear / Of the midnight ride of Paul Revere." — Henry Wadsworth Longfellow

Paul Revere is famous for his "midnight ride" on April 18, 1775. That night Paul warned Massachusetts Patriots that British soldiers were marching out of Boston, ready to attack.

Two years later, on April 26, 1777, young **Sybil** Ludington became the "female Paul Revere" when she warned New York Patriots that British soldiers were preparing an attack.

There were many riders who helped the American colonists in their struggle to become independent from Britain. Paul Revere and Sybil Ludington stand out because of their particularly heroic and dangerous rides.

Riders were important before and during the American Revolution. Communication was slow. There were no telephones, no computers, and no fast mail services. Important messages were carried by daring riders on fast horses.

Paul Revere's first ride came in November 1773. The British had sent ships loaded with tea to Boston. The colonists did not want the tea. The British told the colonists that they would have to pay a tax on the tea if the tea was unloaded. The Americans believed that they should not have to pay this tax. Paul Revere was sent by Patriot

Box of tea thrown into Boston Harbor

leaders to warn other colonists that more ships filled with tea were coming to America.

Paul's second ride came two and a half weeks later, on December 17, 1773. Paul had been up all night with other Patriots, throwing the hated British tea into Boston Harbor. The Patriots needed someone to ride to New York and Philadelphia to spread the word about the "Boston Tea Party."

Paul raced to these two cities. He rode more than sixty miles a day. He covered the seven-hundred-mile round-trip distance in record time. During the Revolution, Paul made rides to New York, to Philadelphia, or to both cities five more times, carrying important messages each time.

But his most famous ride came on the night of April 18, 1775. Two lantern lights hanging in a church tower signaled that the British soldiers were leaving Boston by boat that night. Their goal was to capture Samuel Adams and John Hancock, two Patriot leaders, in Lexington. Then the British would march to Concord to find the guns and ammunition that the Patriots had stored there.

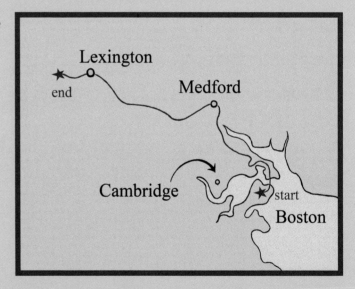

Map of Paul Revere's midnight ride

Paul jumped onto a borrowed horse named Brown Beauty and rode into the night. Later, Paul wrote, "I set off, it was then about 11 o'clock; the Moon shone bright." Two British soldiers tried to stop Paul, but he galloped away from them. Around midnight, Paul reached Lexington. He warned Adams and

Hancock that British soldiers were coming to capture them. Adams and Hancock escaped to safety. Then Paul headed to Concord. As he rode through the countryside, Paul woke people up by calling, "The Regulars [British soldiers] are coming out! The Regulars are coming out!"

Before he could reach Concord, Paul Revere was captured by the British. Later he was released and returned to Lexington. Another rider dashed off to Concord to warn the Patriots that the British were coming.

When the British arrived in Concord, they faced a determined group of American colonists. Gunfire erupted. The British retreated back to Boston. The Revolutionary War had begun. Thanks to Paul Revere and other brave riders, the colonists had been warned, so they were able to defeat the British soldiers.

Door of a local militiaman's house

Two years later, Sybil Ludington had her own chance to ride into history. Sybil was only sixteen years old when she made her heroic ride. Unlike Paul Revere, Sybil was not actively involved in the war, but her father was. He was the leader of a local militia, a group of colonists who would fight when the British came near.

On the night of April 26, 1777, there was a loud knock on the Ludingtons' door. A Patriot messenger told

Colonel Ludington that the British were burning the nearby town of Danbury, Connecticut. Colonel Ludington had to stay home to organize the local militiamen when they gathered at his farm. But who could he send to tell the other militiamen farther away that it was time to assemble?

Sybil volunteered. She was an excellent rider. She knew all the local roads. Colonel Ludington had no choice but to send his oldest daughter on this dangerous mission.

President George Washington

Sybil climbed onto Star, her beloved horse, and galloped into the rainy night. At each house she came to, Sybil hit the door with a strong stick she carried. "The British are burning Danbury! Muster [gather] at Ludington's!" she shouted before dashing off.

Sybil rode forty miles that stormy night. Wet and exhausted, she reached home at dawn. The militiamen she had helped call out cheered Sybil before they marched to fight the British. A few weeks later, Colonel Ludington and his men defeated the British at Ridgefield, Connecticut. George Washington himself thanked Sybil Ludington, the "female Paul Revere," for her brave ride.

Giblin, James. *The Many Rides of Paul Revere*. New York: Scholastic, 2007.
Redmond, Shirley. *Patriots in Petticoats*. New York: Random House, 2004.
Sullivan, George. *Paul Revere*. New York: Scholastic, 1999.

Sacagawea

c.1788–1812

"[Sacagawea] deserved a greater reward for her attention and services on that route than we had in our power to give her."
— **Captain William Clark, August 20, 1806**

Sacagawea and Pomp on a dollar coin

More than two hundred years after the Lewis and Clark expedition reached its end, Sacagawea's name lives on in many places throughout the United States. There's Mount Sacagawea, the Sacagawea River, Sacagawea Glacier, and Sacagawea Peak. There are schools, lakes, and parks named after Sacagawea. There are monuments and statues that honor her. There is even a Sacagawea dollar coin. In 2001, President William J. Clinton made Sacagawea an honorary sergeant in the U.S. Army. Sacagawea is one of the most famous women in American history. But who was Sacagawea, and why do we remember her today?

Sacagawea is famous for her heroic efforts as she traveled more than eight thousand miles with the Lewis and Clark expedition from 1805 to 1806. Sacagawea's courage, determination, and knowledge helped Lewis and Clark achieve their goal of crossing the continent. Without Sacagawea, the expedition might not have been a success.

Sacagawea stepped into history's pages in November 1804, when she met Captain Meriwether Lewis and Captain William Clark. The explorers built Fort Mandan near Sacagawea's home in North Dakota. They spent the winter at Fort Mandan, preparing to complete their journey across America.

Lewis and Clark hired Sacagawea's husband, Toussaint Charbonneau, to join their expedition because he spoke many Native American languages. However, he did not speak Shoshone. Lewis and Clark had to have someone who spoke Shoshone.

They needed to trade for Shoshone horses to help them cross the towering Rocky Mountains. Fortunately, Charbonneau's wife, Sacagawea, spoke this language! So Sacagawea and her infant son, Jean-Baptiste (nicknamed Pomp), also joined the Lewis and Clark expedition. Sacagawea had grown up in the mountains and was excited to go with Lewis and Clark. She would be able to return to her childhood home.

On the morning of April 7, 1805, the expedition left Fort Mandan. Sacagawea soon proved she was an excellent addition to the group. She collected roots, which added vegetables to the men's diet of meat. She taught Captain Lewis the Native American names for plants and animals as they traveled. She helped make camp each night, setting up the tepee and cooking meals. And she cared for baby Pomp, who was a happy reminder to the tired men of their faraway homes and families.

Map showing the route of the Lewis and Clark Trail

The journey up the Missouri River was difficult. The men paddled and poled against the Missouri's rough current. They sailed when they could. The group battled millions of mosquitoes and gnats. Hail pelted them. Thunderstorms drenched them. Grizzly bears attacked them.

One day, Sacagawea was traveling in a small boat with Pomp. Suddenly, a gust of wind hit the boat's sail. The boat tipped and filled with water. Sacagawea made sure Pomp was safe. Then she rescued compasses, books, clothing, and other equipment the expedition needed in order to survive. Captain Lewis and Captain Clark praised Sacagawea's heroic efforts. They named a small river the Sacagawea River in her honor.

Summer was passing quickly, and Lewis and Clark were becoming more and more anxious. They still had not reached the Rocky Mountains. They had to hurry to find the Shoshones and, with Sacagawea's help, trade for the horses they needed. Sacagawea was eager, too. She wanted to see her Shoshone home and family.

One day, Sacagawea recognized Beaverhead Rock. Sacagawea told Lewis and Clark that they were near her people. Finally, the expedition had reached the Shoshone camp high in the mountains. Sacagawea approached the Shoshone chief to trade for the horses. Suddenly, Sacagawea jumped up and hugged the chief. The chief was her brother Cameahwait!

The Pacific Ocean

Even with the horses, the expedition struggled to cross the mountains. At last, they reached the western slope, built canoes, and hurried down the rivers to the sea as best as they could. On November 7, 1805, Captain Clark wrote, "Ocean in view! O the joy!"

The Lewis and Clark expedition and Sacagawea had finally reached the Pacific Ocean. The men built Fort Clatsop, where they spent the long, wet winter. Sacagawea sewed elk-skin clothes and moccasins, cooked elk meat, and collected roots and berries. She even saw a whale wash up on shore. Captain Clark made a map of the areas they had passed through. Captain Lewis wrote in his journals about the people they had met and the adventures they had had.

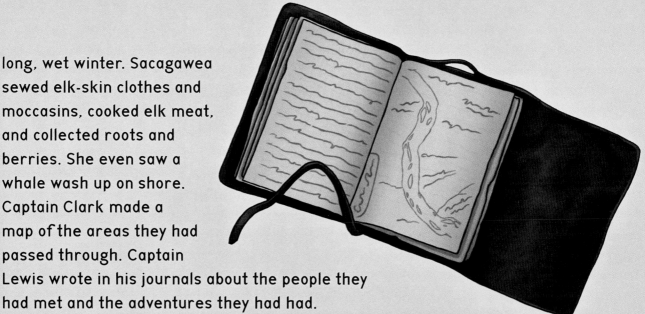

Journal of Captain Meriwether Lewis

In March 1806, the expedition began the long journey home. They paddled up the Columbia River and crossed the Rocky Mountains. Lewis and Clark split up so they could explore more land. Captain Lewis went north. Captain Clark and Sacagawea went south. The two groups planned to meet on the Missouri River. Sacagawea knew this land well. She had often traveled here with her people. She guided Captain Clark, showing him a pass through the mountains.

Lewis and Clark met as they had planned. Now they did not have to battle the mighty Missouri River. Instead, they raced downstream until they reached the Native Americans near Fort Mandan. Here Sacagawea, Pomp, and Charbonneau left Lewis and Clark.

Charbonneau received five hundred dollars for his work. Sacagawea received only praise for all she had done. By finding food, rescuing supplies, making clothes, trading for horses, and leading the way at times, Sacagawea had heroically helped make the Lewis and Clark expedition the great success it was.

Ambrose, Stephen. *Undaunted Courage: Meriwether Lewis, Thomas Jefferson, and the Opening of the American West.* New York: Touchstone, 1996.
Howard, Harold. *Sacajawea.* Norman, OK: University of Oklahoma Press, 1971.
St. George, Judith. *Sacagawea.* New York: G. P. Putnam's Sons, 1997.

Sojourner Truth
c.1797–1883

"The truth is powerful and will prevail." — **Sojourner Truth**

Sojourner Truth

Truth was born a slave around 1797. She never knew her birthday, because slaves' birthdays were often not written down. Her parents named her Isabella. Her last name was that of her owner, Johannes Hardenbergh. One day, Isabella Hardenbergh would become the famous antislavery and women's rights leader Sojourner Truth.

Isabella's parents loved her very much. They all lived on Hardenbergh's farm, near the Hudson River in New York State. Isabella knew only one of her brothers. The rest of her many brothers and sisters had been sold to other owners. Her parents often told her stories about her missing siblings.

When Isabella was nine years old, she was sold to John Neely for one hundred dollars. Mr. Neely was extremely mean to Isabella. In 1810, Isabella was sold to John Dumont. She was Mr. Dumont's slave for sixteen years.

A field Sojourner worked in

Isabella worked hard for her new owner. She plowed, planted, and harvested his fields. Mr. Dumont said, "She could do as much work as half a dozen . . . people." But Isabella did not benefit from her hard labor. She was still a slave.

Because she was a slave, Isabella never had a chance to go to school. She never learned to read or write. She memorized songs and parts of the Bible that she heard. When she was eighteen, Mr. Dumont made Isabella marry Tom, another one of his slaves. Isabella and Tom had five children. As children of slaves, they were slaves, too.

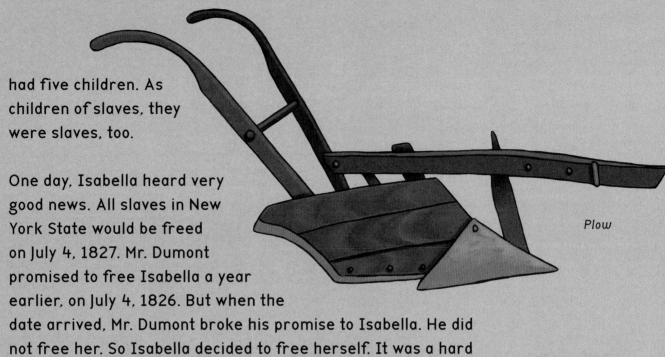

Plow

One day, Isabella heard very good news. All slaves in New York State would be freed on July 4, 1827. Mr. Dumont promised to free Isabella a year earlier, on July 4, 1826. But when the date arrived, Mr. Dumont broke his promise to Isabella. He did not free her. So Isabella decided to free herself. It was a hard decision for Isabella because she could take only one of her children with her. She chose the baby, Sophia, since she was too young to be left behind.

Early one morning, Isabella put Sophia on her hip and walked away as fast as she could. But Mr. Dumont caught up with her. Mr. Dumont claimed that Isabella had run away from him. Isabella said, "No, I did not *run* away; I walked away by day-light, and all because you had promised me a year of my time." A neighbor who disliked slavery said he would pay for Isabella's work for the rest of the year. Mr. Dumont agreed.

On July 4, 1827, Isabella was finally free! Isabella worked for many different people over the next fifteen years. Then, in 1843, Isabella made two big decisions. She began traveling to tell people about God. And she changed her name to Sojourner Truth. She took this name because *sojourner* means "traveler," and she felt that her calling was to spread the truth as she traveled to different places. Sojourner went to religious meetings where she spoke about God. She quoted verses from the Bible. She sang songs people knew and songs she had made up. She listened to other preachers. Sojourner took great joy in having children read the Bible to her.

Several years later, Sojourner met Frederick Douglass, a former slave. Douglass was already famous for his work to end slavery.

Sojourner's book

He was well known for his book about his days as a slave. Sojourner decided she wanted a book about her life. She told her story to a friend who wrote it down. In 1850, Sojourner's book — *The Narrative of Sojourner Truth: A Northern Slave* — was published. Sojourner traveled the country preaching, singing, selling her book, and speaking out against slavery. She often said, "The truth is powerful and will prevail."

Sojourner's life took a new turn around this time. She was invited to speak out for women's rights. Sojourner gave her most important speech on May 28, 1851, at a national women's rights convention in Akron, Ohio. Sojourner said, "I am for a woman's rights. I have as much muscle as any man, and can do as much work as any man. I have plowed and reaped and husked and chopped and mowed." She urged American men to give all American women their rights.

During the Civil War, Sojourner worked to get African Americans the right to fight in the Union Army. She set up a training camp for black soldiers. In Washington, D.C., she helped freed slaves establish new lives. And she visited President Abraham Lincoln

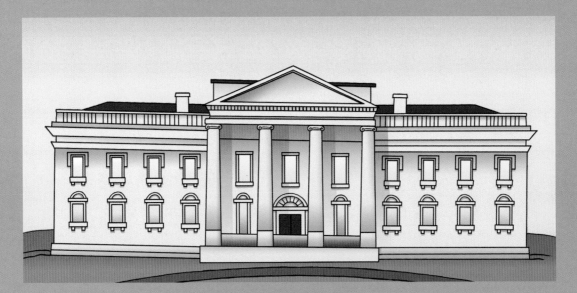

President Abraham Lincoln's White House

in the White House. Later, Sojourner said, "I must say, and I am proud to say, that I never was treated by any one with more kindness and cordiality than were shown to me by that great and good man, Abraham Lincoln."

Sojourner kept battling for equal rights. She won a court battle to integrate Washington's streetcars. When black people and white people finally began riding the streetcars together, Sojourner said, "The inside of the cars looked like pepper and salt."

For the rest of her life, Sojourner dedicated herself to helping others. One day, when she was eighty-six years old, Sojourner told a friend, "I'm going home like a shooting star." On November 26, 1883, Sojourner Truth died in Battle Creek, Michigan.

Sojourner was the best-known African American woman of her time. Born a slave, she refused to remain one. Denied her rights as a woman, she fought to gain them. Sojourner received many honors after her death. But one was especially appropriate. In 1997, the *Sojourner* space rover was launched. Sojourner spoke the truth when she said, "I'm going home like a shooting star."

Roop, Peter, and Connie Roop. *Sojourner Truth*. New York: Scholastic, 2002.
Truth, Sojourner. *Narrative of Sojourner Truth*. Mineola, NY: Dover Publications, 1997.

AFRICAN AMERICAN ANTISLAVERY LEADER

Frederick Douglass

c.1818–1895

"The white man's happiness cannot be purchased by the black man's misery." — Frederick Douglass

Frederick

Frederick Douglass was born in Tuckahoe, Maryland. His mother's name was Harriet Bailey, and Frederick's real name was Frederick Augustus Washington Bailey. He changed his name to Frederick Douglass after he escaped from slavery. As Frederick Douglass, he became the best-known African American antislavery leader in America.

Frederick was raised by his grandmother until the age of six. Then he was separated from her. Frederick's mother lived on another farm, twelve miles away. She rarely got to see her son. Frederick's mother died when he was only seven years old. Frederick never knew his father.

Young Frederick worked on his owner's farm. He brought the cows to their barn in the evening. He chased chickens out of the garden. He cleaned the yard and ran errands. But he was often hungry and cold. He had no shoes, socks, pants, or jacket. He wore a long shirt that reached to his knees. On winter nights, Frederick stole a large cloth bag and slept in it.

Frederick went to live in Baltimore when he was eight years old. He was still a slave, but he had more freedom. And he had his first pair of pants! Frederick's life changed in another way at this time. He discovered reading and writing. His new mistress even taught him a few letters and how to spell some short words. But her husband thought that teaching

One of Frederick's copy-books: pavement and chalk

Frederick would spoil him as a slave. And teaching a slave to read was against the law.

Frederick was determined to learn to read. He learned more letters from his young white friends. Later, as an author, Frederick wrote, "During this time, my copy-book was the board fence, brick wall, and pavement; my pen and ink was a lump of chalk." From these difficult beginnings, Frederick would go on to write three books and work on a number of newspapers, including two he started.

In Baltimore, Frederick saw African Americans who were not slaves. They were free to live their own lives. Frederick began to dream about being free himself. He wrote, "I was now about twelve years old, and the thought of being a *slave for life* began to bear heavily upon my heart." Unfortunately, Frederick was sent to another farm to work. He hated and rebelled against it. Mr. Covey, the farmer, beat him.

One day when Mr. Covey hit him, Frederick fought back. The men battled for two hours. Mr. Covey never hit Frederick again. Frederick wrote, "This battle with Mr. Covey was the turning-point in my career as a slave." Frederick tried to escape twice, but was caught. On his third try, dressed as a sailor, Frederick escaped to New Bedford, Massachusetts. Although officially he still belonged to his owner, Frederick was free at last.

A sailor hat and shirt

To keep Mr. Covey from finding him, Frederick changed his last name from Bailey to Stanley to Johnson and finally to Douglass.

In Massachusetts, Frederick read the *Liberator*, a newspaper dedicated to ending slavery. He realized that many people were working to end slavery. One day, Frederick spoke at an antislavery rally. He talked about his life as a slave and his daring escape. People were excited by what Frederick said. Frederick spoke at more meetings. More people heard him. Some people, however, did not believe that an escaped slave could read and speak as well as Frederick Douglass did. They doubted he had ever been a slave. So, in 1845, he wrote *Narrative of the Life of Frederick Douglass, An American Slave*. More people read Frederick's story and joined the fight against slavery.

Narrative of the Life of Frederick Douglass, An American Slave

Written by Himself.

Frederick's autobiography

Frederick's popularity brought danger. Because Frederick was so well known, he worried that his owner in Maryland would find him and take him back into slavery. Frederick went to England, where slavery had been abolished. He gave many more speeches. In 1846, English friends raised seven hundred and fifty dollars to buy Frederick's freedom. At last, Frederick Douglass was truly free.

Frederick returned to America and continued his antislavery work. He gave more speeches stating that "the white man's happiness cannot be purchased by the black man's misery." He started the *North Star* newspaper to write against slavery. He spoke and wrote about equal rights for women, too. He and his family ran a station on the Underground Railroad in Rochester, New York, to help slaves escape to freedom. During the Civil War, Frederick met with President Abraham Lincoln. He urged Lincoln to free the slaves and to let African Americans join the Union army.

ROCHESTER, NY

Map showing where Frederick and his family ran an Underground Railroad station in Rochester, NY

In 1863, President Lincoln freed all slaves in states that were fighting against the Union. Lincoln also let African Americans join the army and navy. Almost two hundred thousand African American soldiers fought for the Union, including two of Frederick's own sons.

In 1865, the Civil War ended, and all African Americans were free. Frederick's hard work to end slavery was finished, so he fought to make sure African Americans had equal rights. Frederick Douglass was the most famous African American leader of his time. He held jobs in Washington, D.C. He was a minister of the United States to Haiti and the Dominican Republic.

On February 20, 1895, Frederick Douglass died. In 1899, a statue of Frederick Douglass was unveiled in Rochester, New York. This is said to be the first monument to an African American man in the United States, a fitting tribute to a person who escaped slavery and became a leader for all Americans.

Douglass, Frederick. *Narrative of the Life of Frederick Douglass*. Cheswold, DE: Prestwick House, 2004.
Elliot, Henry. *Frederick Douglass: From Slavery to Statesman*. New York: Crabtree Publishing, 2010.
Sterngass, Jon. *Frederick Douglass*. New York: Chelsea House, 2009.

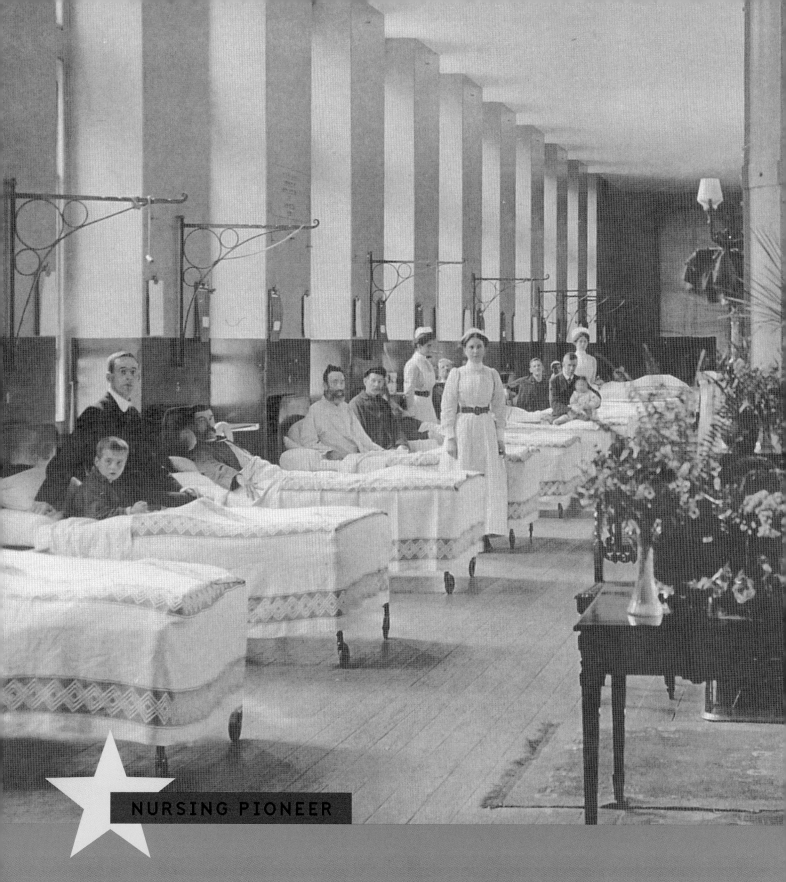

Florence Nightingale

1820–1910

"But it must be done." — **Florence Nightingale**

Florence Nightingale was born on May 12, 1820. She was named Florence because her parents were visiting Florence, Italy, at the time. The Nightingale family returned to England the next year.

Florence spent her childhood at the Nightingales' large home in Hampshire, England. Florence did not go to school. Instead, her parents hired a governess to teach her and her sister, Parthe, to read, write, draw, and do needlework at home.

Later, Mr. Nightingale taught the girls Greek, Latin, French, Italian, and German. He taught them history and math. Florence's mother taught them how to run a household, too. Florence studied hard and was especially good at math. At a time when only wealthy children got an education, their schooling prepared Florence and Parthe for the future.

But Florence also liked to daydream. In her imagination, she had exciting adventures and changed the world. From the time she was six years old, Florence wanted to use her skills. *What good is my education*, she wondered, *if I can't use it to make the world better?*

Books that Florence studied from

"The first thought I can remember, and the last, was nursing work," Florence later wrote. Florence helped sick relatives whenever she could. She cooked good food for them, read to them, and talked with them. She took food, clothes, and medicine to poor people.

But Florence's parents did not want Florence to become a nurse. They wanted her to marry and settle down. Once, when Florence asked if she could spend three months studying at a hospital, her parents became very angry. Florence's mother was so upset by Florence's desire to become a nurse that she said, "We are ducks who have hatched a wild swan."

Medicine

But Florence was stubborn. She wanted to care for sick people. Secretly, at night, she began reading about hospitals by candlelight. She wrote to friends about health care. She tried to figure out why people were dying.

At this time, there were no female doctors in England. No one knew that germs made people sick. No one realized that if a doctor only washed his hands, he would not spread sickness to his patients.

Florence visited a hospital in Germany. Her parents were furious. In 1851, stubborn Florence told her parents she was going back to the hospital in Germany and they couldn't stop her.

Florence's visit to the hospital changed her life. Florence worked long hours with little food. She observed patients. She watched doctors in action. She made notes on how to better organize the hospital.

In 1853, when she was thirty-three years old, Florence's hard work paid off. She got a job in a London hospital with only twenty-five patients. Florence could nurse, but she wouldn't be paid. Although her father disapproved, he gave her money. Florence immediately improved the hospital. She bought better food at cheaper prices. She saved money on drugs. She made sheets and covers for beds.

Another big change came in 1854, when England joined Turkey in a war against Russia. Thousands of British soldiers went to fight. Many soldiers were wounded. Others got sick. But the hospitals for the men were horrible. There was little food. Everything was filthy. The soldiers had no warm clothes in winter. Medical supplies were scarce. Something had to be done.

One British government leader knew Florence's work. He suggested that she go to Turkey as superintendent of nurses. With some of her own money, clothes, and medical supplies, and with thirty-eight nurses she had picked herself, Florence Nightingale sailed to Turkey.

Florence had seen bad hospitals before, but nothing had prepared her for what she found in Turkey. Thousands of sick or wounded soldiers were crowded into rooms crawling with lice, mice, rats, fleas, and cockroaches. There was a shortage of clean water to drink and to wash wounds with. Few men had blankets or even beds. The soldiers had only hard bread and spoiled meat to eat.

Florence and her nurses cleaned the hospital. They got better water and prepared better food. They found knives, forks, soap, and toothbrushes for the men. They let fresh air into the hospital. They sent for books for the men and even found teachers to teach those who couldn't read. They had two dead horses removed from the sewer.

Florence's lamp

Every night, Florence walked through the hospital helping her patients. The grateful soldiers called her the Lady with the Lamp. Soon fewer soldiers were dying from sickness or infected wounds. Before Florence had arrived, forty-two out of every one hundred soldiers in the hospital had died. After Florence's improvements, only two out of one hundred died!

Florence became famous. Queen Victoria wrote to her and talked with her. People gave money to build the Nightingale Training School for Nurses. One songwriter wrote, "May God give her strength, and her heart never fail, / One of Heaven's best gifts is Miss Nightingale."

Florence helped start the Red Cross and Red Crescent organizations, which today help millions of people around the world combat disease and improve their living conditions. She inspired thousands of women and men to become nurses. Florence helped others begin nursing schools using her methods. She wrote books and articles to improve hospital conditions worldwide.

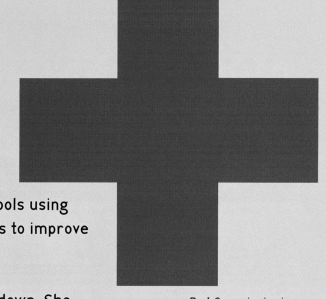

Red Cross insignia

Her years of heroic effort wore Florence down. She became sick herself. But she continued urging governments to improve people's lives.

Florence died peacefully on August 13, 1910. Thousands of nurses, soldiers, and other admirers attended her memorial service at St. Paul's Cathedral in London. Florence Nightingale was buried near her childhood home in Hampshire, England.

Barnham, Kay. *Florence Nightingale*. New York: Raintree, 2003.
Gorrell, Gena. *Heart and Soul: The Story of Florence Nightingale*. Toronto: Tundra Books, 2000.
Strachey, Lytton. *The Biography of Florence Nightingale*. Radford, VA: A & D Publishing, 2008.

Mohandas Gandhi

1869–1948

"I want world sympathy in this battle of Right against Might."

— Mohandas Gandhi

Mohandas Gandhi was born on October 2, 1869, in India. At that time, India was ruled by Great Britain, an island nation approximately five thousand miles away. After a long struggle led by Gandhi, India became an independent nation in 1947.

Gandhi was very shy when he was young. He ran to school so he would not have to talk to anyone. Gandhi said, "My books and my lessons were my sole companions."

Gandhi felt safe and loved at home. His father taught him to respect all people, no matter their religion. The Gandhis were Hindus, but many of Gandhi's father's friends were Muslims. From his mother, Gandhi learned that keeping his word was the most important thing a person could do.

Gandhi went to high school when he was twelve years old. He learned to read English, write English, and speak English. He won prizes for his schoolwork. Gandhi did not like to play sports, but he enjoyed long walks.

Gandhi's life changed when he was thirteen. His parents arranged for him to be married! Gandhi's young bride was named Kasturba. Gandhi and Kasturba stayed married until she died more than sixty years later. They raised four sons together.

Kasturba Gandhi

Gandhi finished high school in 1887 and went to England to become a lawyer. In 1893, Gandhi went to South Africa to work in a law firm. South Africa changed Gandhi's life. There he learned the leadership skills he needed to peacefully guide India to independence.

One day, Gandhi was riding a train. He had a first-class ticket. A white man refused to ride with the brown-skinned Gandhi. Gandhi would not move and was pushed off the train. After this experience, Gandhi promised to fight for the rights of Indians in South Africa. And he did. He wrote newspaper articles protesting discrimination against people of color. He demanded equal treatment under the law. Gandhi gained a lot of support for his views and began to build a strong following.

Gandhi believed he could peacefully change unfair laws. He called his nonviolent idea satyagraha, which means "truth and firmness." Gandhi and thousands of his followers were put in jail for these beliefs. But, finally the government did change many of the unfair laws.

Gandhi was a hero when he returned to India in 1915. He was called Mahatma, or "Great Soul," for his work in South Africa. Gandhi decided to use satyagraha to help Indians gain their independence from Britain.

Gandhi traveled around India meeting people. He spun his own cotton to make his clothes. He peacefully helped farmers get fair pay for their crops.

He helped factory workers get paid more, too. Gandhi vowed not to eat until the workers got better pay. Newspapers told Gandhi's story. Millions of people worried about Gandhi's health. Finally, the factory owners gave in. Fasting became part of Gandhi's nonviolent satyagraha movement.

In 1921, Gandhi became head of the Indian National Congress.

Spinning wheel

He and his followers worked to peacefully gain self-rule for India. Gandhi encouraged Indians to weave their own cotton clothes so they wouldn't have to buy expensive British cloth. Each day, Gandhi spun yards of thread on a spinning wheel. Gandhi's simple spinning wheel became a symbol of the Indian struggle for self-rule. Today, the shape of a spinning wheel is on India's flag.

India's flag with the shape of a spinning wheel in its center

The British rulers, however, were upset with the independence movement. Gandhi and thousands of his peaceful followers were put in jail for their protests against the British. Gandhi read when he was in jail. He wrote. He prayed. He spun cotton thread. And he fasted. Once he went without food for twenty-one days. People around the world were again concerned about Gandhi's health.

Gandhi knew he had to highlight India's struggle for independence, so he decided to peacefully protest British salt laws. These laws made it illegal for Indians to make or sell salt. Indians had to buy expensive British salt, even though free sea salt could be gathered at the seashore.

Gandhi walked 240 miles to the coast. Thousands of Indians joined him on his Salt March. People around the world followed Gandhi's heroic march to the sea. Gandhi reached the shore and picked up sea salt. Before long, he and fifty thousand of his followers were jailed for breaking the salt laws. Gandhi said, "I want world sympathy in this battle of Right against Might."

Slowly, Gandhi's right overcame Britain's might. India finally became independent on August 15, 1947. Over the decades of struggle, Gandhi spent 2,089 days in Indian jails.

Gandhi holding salt during the Salt March

Despite the victory of independence, however, Gandhi was saddened. For years, he had peacefully fought for a united India. Instead, India was split into two countries — India and Pakistan. Most Hindus would live in India. Most Muslims would live in Pakistan.

Unfortunately, not all Indians supported Gandhi. On January 30, 1948, Gandhi was assassinated. Gandhi, who believed in nonviolence, had died violently. One Indian leader said, "Our beloved leader, Bapu [Papa] as we called him, the Father of the Nation, is no more. . . . The light has gone out."

But Gandhi's light still burns brightly. Dr. Martin Luther King, Jr., used Gandhi's nonviolent teachings to guide the civil rights movement in America. Nelson Mandela used Gandhi's nonviolent approach to end the hated apartheid that kept black and white people separated in South Africa. Gandhi's use of nonviolence to gain India's independence proved to the world that right was indeed stronger than might.

Gandhi, Mohandas. *An Autobiography: The Story of My Experiments with Truth.* Boston: Beacon Press, 1993.
Pastan, Amy. *Gandhi: A Photographic Story of a Life.* New York: DK Publishing, 2006.

SOLDIER, AUTHOR, POLITICIAN

Winston Churchill

1874–1965

"I have nothing to offer but blood, toil, tears, and sweat."

— Winston Churchill

Winston Churchill was born on November 30, 1874, at Blenheim Palace in England. Randolph Churchill, his father, was English. Jennie Jerome Churchill, his mother, was American.

Winston's parents loved him, but they did not spend much time with him as he was growing up. His father worked hard as a political leader. His mother was busy with her intense social life. At home, young Winston was raised mostly by Mrs. Anne Everest, his beloved nanny.

When he was seven years old, Winston went away to boarding school. He saw his family only on school vacations. Winston liked to learn, but he didn't like school. Math was especially hard for him. However, he did like books. *Treasure Island* was one of his favorites. This exciting book inspired him to read more challenging books.

Winston went to Harrow, a famous school in England, when he was thirteen years old. He struggled with his schoolwork, but his English teacher, Mr. Somervell, did teach him to write well. And he excelled in the sport of fencing.

Fencing equipment

As a young boy, Winston also enjoyed playing with his toy soldiers. He arranged them in battle formation and fought imaginary wars. Winston's military interest continued into his teenage years, so he went to the Royal Military College in Sandhurst, England.

Winston graduated from Sandhurst with honors in 1894 and became a cavalry officer. But, he wanted more action in his life, which he found as a journalist. There was a war going on in Cuba, and Winston went there to write articles about it for a London newspaper. On his twenty-first birthday, a bullet almost hit Winston while he was eating! That was Winston's first taste of war.

Winston was very busy for the next twenty years. He fought in India, Egypt, and South Africa. He was captured by enemies and escaped. He wrote books and newspaper articles. He made speeches. He was elected to Parliament. He got married and had children. He became the First Lord of the Admiralty and was responsible for improving the British navy. He took flying lessons. He began painting pictures.

During World War I (1914–1918), Winston served in the British government, but he also led troops fighting in France. After the war, Winston worked both in and out of the government, and he continued speaking, writing, and painting.

As the years went by, Winston became increasingly worried about the stronghold Adolf Hitler, the dictator of Germany, was gaining in Europe. Winston worked hard to increase the number of airplanes and ships that Britain had. He firmly believed that Germany had to be stopped from invading and taking over other

Map showing distance between the United Kingdom and Germany

countries. In 1939, World War II broke out. Winston became prime minister of England in 1940. He had been chosen to lead Britain in the war against Germany.

Winston used his skill with words to inspire his nation. In one speech, he said, "I have nothing to offer but blood, toil, tears, and sweat" to protect Britain from Germany. Winston's goal was to rally Britain "to wage war, by sea, land and air, with all our might."

The road to victory in World War II was long and hard. Germany conquered most of Europe, leaving Britain to stand alone and face a German invasion. Brave British pilots defended their country from the air during the Battle of Britain. British citizens lived through long nights of German bombing, called the Blitz.

To rally his country, Winston said, "What is our aim? I can answer in one word: Victory! Victory at all costs, victory in spite of all terror, victory however long and hard the road may be." He worked hard to get arms and supplies from other countries. He made plans to win the war. He traveled to meet other leaders.

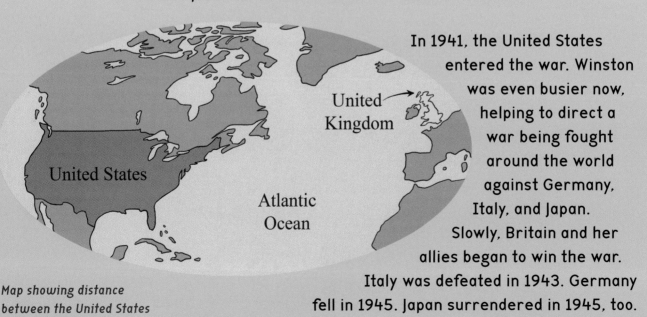

United Kingdom

United States

Atlantic Ocean

Map showing distance between the United States and the United Kingdom

In 1941, the United States entered the war. Winston was even busier now, helping to direct a war being fought around the world against Germany, Italy, and Japan. Slowly, Britain and her allies began to win the war. Italy was defeated in 1943. Germany fell in 1945. Japan surrendered in 1945, too.

When peace with Germany was announced, Winston told his grateful nation, "This is *your* victory." But without Winston's unique blend of wit, wisdom, energy, and determination, Britain and her allies might not have won the war.

Winston served his nation and the world for many years after the end of World War II. He spoke out against the dangers of communism. He wrote a history of World War II. In 1951, he became prime minister again. In 1953, he was knighted by Queen Elizabeth II and became Sir Winston Churchill. He won the Nobel Prize in Literature for his books and his speeches. He worked for individual freedoms and defended human rights. In 1963, President Kennedy made Winston an honorary citizen of the United States. He was the first person ever to receive this honor.

Nobel Prize in Literature

Winston died on January 24, 1965. More than one hundred thousand people paid their respects to him as they passed by his coffin. Queen Elizabeth II came to say farewell to the man who so heroically fought for freedom by serving in the military and in the government and who inspired the world with his words.

Johnson, Paul. *Churchill.* New York: Viking, 2009.
Keegan, John. *Winston Churchill.* New York: Viking, 2002.
Severance, John. *Winston Churchill: Soldier, Statesman, Artist.* New York: Clarion Books, 1996.

Rosa Parks

1913–2005

"It was time for someone to stand up — or in my case, sit down.
I refused to move." — **Rosa Parks**

Rosa

Rosa Parks was born Rosa McCauley on February 4, 1913, in Tuskegee, Alabama. Her happy parents had no idea that tiny Rosa would one day change history.

Map showing Pine Level, Alabama

Rosa grew up in her grandparents' home in Pine Level, Alabama. Her father, a carpenter, left the family when Rosa was young. Her mother taught school a few miles away and came home on weekends.

Rosa enjoyed living with her grandparents. Rosa's grandmother taught her to cook, plant and harvest their garden, and sew. Her grandfather took her fishing, told her stories, and taught Rosa to stand up for herself. "I was a person with dignity and self-respect," Rosa said. "My grandfather was the one who instilled in my mother and her sisters, and in their children, that you don't put up with bad treatment from anybody."

Rosa went to school when she was six. Her school was only for African American children. Black and white children could not go to the same school when Rosa was growing up in Alabama. The schools were separate, and not equal.

Rosa's school had one room for about sixty students. There were no desks, and only a few used books. The windows had no glass. It was hard to do work in such a crowded room, with so few supplies, so Rosa learned many lessons outside of school. She learned there were laws that kept African Americans and white people apart. Black people could not sit in restaurants with white people. Black children could not play in parks or swim in pools with white children. There were "White-Only" and "Colored-Only" water fountains.

Rosa believed everyone was equal. She knew the laws that were keeping black and white people "separate but equal" were wrong. Rosa hoped someday these laws would change.

When Rosa was in eleventh grade, her grandmother got sick. Rosa really wanted to finish high school. She wanted to be a teacher like her mother.

Drinking fountains for white people and black people

But Rosa made a difficult decision and left school to take care of her grandmother. She also worked on her grandparents' farm, sewed shirts, and cleaned the homes of white people.

Rosa met Raymond Parks when she was nineteen. His friends called him Parks. Soon Rosa was calling him Parks, too. Rosa liked him because "Parks believed in being a man and expected to be treated as a man."

Rosa married Parks in 1932. She now went by Rosa Parks, a name that would echo in history. Rosa and Parks lived in Montgomery, Alabama. Rosa finished high school. But Rosa

Rosa's sewing machine

couldn't find a teaching job, so she sewed clothes at the Montgomery Fair department store.

Rosa rode the bus to work and back home again. Each time she got on the bus, Rosa paid her dime and took a seat in the back where the law said African Americans had to sit. Rosa knew this law was wrong, but she and other African Americans felt helpless. Each bus driver carried a gun to enforce the law.

On December 1, 1955, Rosa had been working hard at her job all day. Christmas was coming and the store was busy. After work, Rosa shopped and thought about the meeting she had planned for that evening. When her bus pulled up, Rosa paid her dime and took her seat near the back of the bus.

More people got on the bus and soon it was crowded. A white man got on and saw that there were no empty seats. The bus driver told Rosa to stand up and give the white man her seat.

Rosa was tired from working all day. But Rosa Parks was also tired of putting up with the unfair treatment of African Americans. Rosa said, "I was just plain tired. It was time for someone to stand up — or in my case, sit down. I refused to move."

The angry bus driver called the police. Rosa was taken to jail. Later that night, her friends got Rosa out of jail. Rosa was told she must go to court on Monday, December 5.

Many people in the African American community in Montgomery heard about Rosa's heroic stand. They decided to stop riding the buses until the law changed so that black people did not have to sit in the back of the bus or give up their seats to white people. A young preacher named Martin Luther King, Jr., helped lead this bus boycott. For the next 381 days, African Americans walked, biked, or rode wagons to work. They carpooled. Soon the buses stopped running because they had so few customers.

Finally, in December 1956, the United States Supreme Court ordered that the buses be fully integrated. No longer would African Americans have to give up their seats to white people or sit in the back of the bus.

Martin Luther King, Jr.'s leadership propelled him to the front of the civil rights movement. But it was shy, quiet, determined Rosa Parks who had the courage to stand up against the unfair laws. Rosa's heroic decision to stay seated on the bus that day changed history.

Boycott signs from the protest in Montgomery, Alabama

Brinkley, Douglas. *Rosa Parks: A Life.* New York: Viking Penguin, 2000.
Parks, Rosa. *Rosa Parks: My Story.* With Jim Haskins. New York: Puffin Books, 1992.

SCIENTIST WHO CONQUERED POLIO

Jonas Salk

1914–1995

"Hope lies in dreams, in imagination and in the courage of those who dare to make dreams into reality." — **Jonas Salk**

Jonas Salk was born on October 28, 1914, in New York City. In 1916, when Jonas was not yet two years old, American parents grew very worried about a disease called polio. Polio attacks a person's muscles, making walking, and even breathing, difficult and dangerous. That year, over nine thousand people had polio in New York City. Twenty-five hundred polio victims died.

The Salks were worried because polio seemed to strike children more often than adults. Most polio victims in New York City were under five years old. The Salks certainly did not want young Jonas to catch polio.

Doctors knew that a virus caused polio. But no one knew how to stop the polio virus from spreading. Mrs. Salk was determined to keep polio out of her home. She made certain Jonas was very clean. She rinsed his mouth and nose with salt and water. She fed her family a balanced diet. And, she limited their servings of meat and sugar, since these foods were thought to make people more susceptible to disease. She also kept Jonas away from other children, who might have carried the dreaded polio virus. Jonas Salk was lucky. He did not get polio. And one day, Jonas would help eliminate the polio virus that had harmed so many people.

A balanced meal

Jonas studied hard in school and spent his spare time reading. Jonas worked so hard that he went to high school when he was only twelve years old. He finished high school when he was fifteen and went to college. At first, Jonas thought he might become a lawyer, but he changed his mind and decided to become a doctor.

In medical school, Jonas enjoyed researching diseases, so he chose to become a medical researcher. Instead of helping to cure someone who already had a disease, Jonas would try to stop the disease from harming more people.

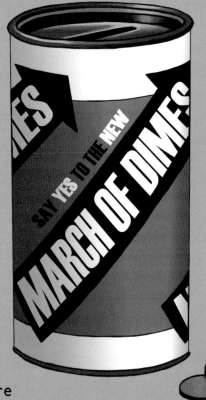

March of Dimes
fundraising container

In 1938, a fundraising campaign called the March of Dimes began to raise money to fight polio. Research doctors needed laboratories and equipment to use in their search to find a way to stop polio. Dimes were mailed to the White House because President Roosevelt himself was a victim of polio. Dimes were collected in buckets at movie theaters. Contests were held to see which communities could raise the most money.

"How many dimes in a mile?" radio stations asked. It took ninety thousand dimes, worth nine thousand dollars, to make a mile of dimes. People lined up dimes along miles of their local sidewalks. In 1938 alone, the March of Dimes raised almost two million dollars. More than fifty laboratories and universities joined the effort to cure polio.

Dr. Jonas Salk graduated from medical school in 1939. At first, he worked on a vaccine to stop the flu. He hadn't focused his attention on polio yet. But in 1950, Jonas, now head of a lab at the University of Pittsburgh in Pennsylvania, decided to join the battle against polio. He pushed hard to obtain grant money so that he could work more directly on the polio vaccine.

Jonas knew there were three types of polio viruses. He also understood that every day our white blood cells battle against germs and infections that might harm us. Jonas's idea was to kill each type of virus to make his vaccine. He thought that if a person was injected with a bit of the dead virus, his or her body would start to fight back. During the fight against the virus, the body would build up the white blood cells it needed to fight a living polio virus. If Dr. Salk's idea worked, people who had the polio vaccine would be immune to polio.

Less than two years after Jonas got his grant money, he had a vaccine that protected monkeys against polio. The big question now was, would his vaccine work to protect humans? Jonas did not want too many people to know about his work. He did not want parents to get their hopes up about a polio vaccine that could protect their children.

Soon, Jonas began testing his vaccine on people. He gave them his polio shots. He ran tests on their blood to see if they were protected against polio. And they were! Jonas was now so sure of his polio vaccine that he gave the shots to himself, his wife, and their three sons.

Newspaper headline announcing
Salk's polio vaccine

Before long, other people heard about Jonas's discovery. Americans everywhere wanted the vaccine for their children. But first, Jonas and other doctors tested more children. The vaccine worked on almost all the children! One newspaper headline read, "SALK'S VACCINE WORKS!"

Not everyone agreed that Jonas's polio vaccine was the best way to stop polio. Other methods were tried, and they worked, too. But over the years, Jonas's vaccine proved to be the best solution.

Jonas turned his attention to other diseases at his new research center, the Salk Institute for Biological Studies. There, he and other researchers made important discoveries about diseases. To honor his heroic efforts, Jonas's words were carved into stone at the Salk Institute: "Hope lies in dreams, in imagination and in the courage of those who dare to make dreams into reality."

Salk Institute

Jonas's dream of conquering polio came true. Today, there are only about one to two thousand new cases of polio worldwide each year. Maybe one day there will be none.

Kluger, Jeffrey. *Splendid Solution: Jonas Salk and the Conquest of Polio*. New York: G. P. Putnam's Sons, 2004.
McPherson, Stephanie. *Jonas Salk: Conquering Polio*. Minneapolis: Lerner, 2002.
Tocci, Salvatore. *Jonas Salk: Creator of the Polio Vaccine*. Berkeley Heights, NJ: Enslow, 2003.

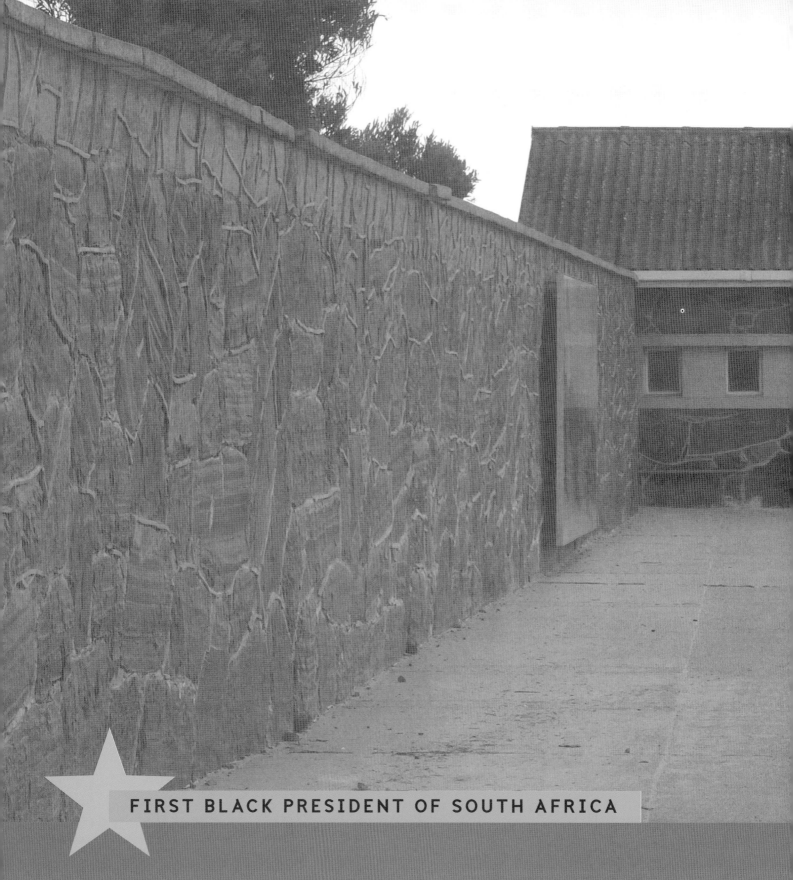

Nelson Mandela

1918–present

"Today is a day like no other before it. Voting in our first free and fair election has begun. Today marks the dawn of our freedom."
— **Nelson Mandela**

Nelson Mandela was born on July 18, 1918, in South Africa. Nelson's parents named him Rolihlahla. *Rolihlahla* means "tree shaker." Nelson Mandela once wrote that he was more of a "troublemaker" than a "tree shaker." After a long struggle, the "trouble" Nelson Mandela made changed South Africa.

Nelson

grew up in a village called Qunu. When Nelson was five, he looked after the sheep and calves grazing on the green hillsides. He gathered honey, fruits, and roots to eat. He swam and fished. He made animals and birds out of clay. He created toys out of twigs and branches. Nelson said, "Nature was our playground."

Honey

Nelson was seven when he went to school. No one else in his family had ever been to school. Instead of calling her students by their real African names, his teacher gave each new student an English name. Rolihlahla Mandela became Nelson Mandela. But Nelson was still a "tree shaker" inside.

Nelson's father died when Nelson was nine years old. Nelson went to live in the chief's village. He spoke the Xhosa language at home, but at school he learned to read and write in English. He studied Xhosa, geography, and history.

Nelson was very observant. He watched how the tribal leaders settled arguments. He saw how they made decisions. He listened as men gave their opinions in an open, democratic way.

But the democracy Nelson saw was only within his own tribe. Although most South Africans were black, a small number of white people controlled the country. Many strict laws kept black people and white people apart. This system of segregation was called apartheid, which means "separateness."

FOR USE BY WHITE PERSONS

THESE PUBLIC PREMISES AND THE AMENITIES THEREOF HAVE BEEN RESERVED FOR THE EXCLUSIVE USE OF WHITE PERSONS.

By Order Provincial Secretary

VIR GEBRUIK DEUR BLANKES

HIERDIE OPENBARE PERSEEL EN DIE GERIEWE DAARVAN IS VIR DIE UITSLUITLIKE GERBRUIK VAN BLANKES AANGEWYS.

Op Las Provinsaile Sekretaries

Sign keeping blacks out of white-only areas

Throughout South Africa, black people and white people lived separately. They lived in different parts of the towns. Black people were often forced to live in "homelands," or black-only areas. Black people rode on "Native-Only" buses. Few black Africans went to school like Nelson did.

Nelson moved to Johannesburg in 1942. He studied hard and became a lawyer. But Nelson was frustrated by how he and other blacks were being treated. They had to carry special passes. They were paid low wages for working in dangerous gold mines and at other hard jobs. They couldn't travel freely. There were very few schools for them. Nelson and other blacks felt they were second-class citizens in their own country.

Nelson learned how Mohandas Gandhi had helped Indian people in South Africa and India. Nelson joined nonviolent protests. He became a member of the African National Congress, a group that worked to gain more rights for black South Africans. But the white-controlled South African government made even harsher laws. One night, Nelson saw police officers shoot and kill eighteen peaceful black protesters. "That day was a turning point in my life," Nelson wrote.

Nelson fought harder for equal rights. He was put in jail. Over a period of five months, eight thousand other blacks were jailed for protesting the government's strict apartheid laws.

Nelson's jail cell

When he was released from jail, the government cracked down on him even more. Nelson couldn't travel or give speeches. He couldn't work with the African National Congress.

In 1964, the South African government put Nelson on trial for planning violent acts against it. Nelson told the court, "I have dedicated myself to this struggle of the African people. . . . I have cherished the ideal of a democratic and free society in which all persons live together in harmony and with equal opportunities."

Nelson was found guilty. He was sentenced to life in prison. There, Nelson broke rocks for roads. He sewed clothes. He read. He studied. He discussed politics. And he fought for his rights and the rights of all South Africans.

The rest of the world saw just how horrible apartheid was. Countries pressured the South African government to change. Pressure from South Africans themselves grew stronger.

Newspaper headline on the day Nelson was freed

Nelson was the symbol for change in South Africa. He became the most famous prisoner in the world. People everywhere from America to India demanded that Nelson be freed.

Finally, on February 11, 1990, Nelson became a free man. He had been in prison for twenty-seven years! Nelson had won his battle, but he continued to fight for equal rights for all South Africans.

Many whites didn't want to give up their power. Slowly, black South Africans gained more rights. Finally, under the brave leadership of F. W. de Klerk, the South African government agreed to have democratic elections. "Today is a day like no other before it," Nelson said. "Voting in our first free and fair election has begun. Today marks the dawn of our freedom." For the first time, black South Africans could vote in their own country.

On April 27, 1994, Nelson was elected president of South Africa. Nelson and F. W. de Klerk received the Nobel Peace Prize for their work. Nelson "Tree Shaker" Mandela had shaken the tree of South Africa and changed the world.

Brown, Laaren, and Lenny Hort. *Nelson Mandela: A Photographic Story of a Life*. New York: DK Publishing, 2006.
Keller, Bill. *Tree Shaker: The Story of Nelson Mandela*. Boston: Kingfisher, 2008.
Mandela, Nelson. *Long Walk to Freedom: The Autobiography of Nelson Mandela*. Boston: Little, Brown, 1995.

Neil Armstrong

1930–present

"That's one small step for man, one giant leap for mankind."

— Neil Armstrong

Neil Armstrong was born on his grandparents' farm near Wapakoneta, Ohio, on August 5, 1930. The Armstrongs admired Neil from head to foot. Who would have guessed that Neil's left foot would be the first human foot to ever step on the moon?

Neil's parents took him to Cleveland to see his first airplanes when he was two years old. Neil enjoyed hearing the roaring engines and seeing the spinning propellers. He watched in wonder as airplanes zoomed overhead. He stared at the planes as they took off and landed. When it was time to leave, Neil begged, "One more, one more." That morning, Neil Armstrong took the first steps on his journey to the moon.

Neil had an amazing adventure when he was six years old. He flew in a plane for the first time! The plane ride lasted only fifteen minutes, but it changed Neil's life forever. Neil's mother said, "I think his love for flying started that day."

Neil's fascination with airplanes soared. He read books about flying, and he especially enjoyed reading about the Wright brothers. Neil began building model airplanes. He wanted to understand how each plane part worked, so he built his planes on his own, not from a kit. He made a model of the first plane he had flown in. He even built a plane with twelve propellers! Neil's mother encouraged her son's hobby. Soon his model planes "flew" from ceilings throughout the house.

Neil's parents gave him a telescope on his ninth birthday. Neil gazed at the stars and the moon. One

Neil's boyhood telescope

friend said, "I imagine he was thinking about the day he would fly into space himself." Mr. Zint, a neighbor, had a big telescope of his own, and he taught Neil more about the night sky. "I do believe the moon was Neil's point of interest right from the start," Mr. Zint said.

Neil studied hard in school, especially math and science. He also worked hard at jobs outside of school, because he had a plan. He would learn how to fly! Flying lessons cost nine dollars an hour. Neil had to work twenty-two hours on the ground to pay for each lesson in the air.

On his sixteenth birthday, Neil got up early. He eagerly rode his bike to the airport. First he passed the written flying test. Then he bravely took off alone, flew, and landed safely. He didn't have a license to drive yet, but Neil Armstrong now had a license to fly!

Neil went to college at Purdue University in Indiana, one of the best engineering schools in the country. Neil took every math, science, and aviation class he could. Two years later, Neil became a fighter pilot in the U.S. Navy. Being a fighter pilot was dangerous, but Neil was excited because now he would fly jets.

Neil flew combat missions during the Korean War. He bombed bridges, shot at enemies, and attacked enemy supply lines. One day, Neil's plane was hit by enemy gunfire. Neil used his skills to keep his plane from crashing. However, Neil had to bail out. But his parachute didn't open all the way!

Fighter plane Neil flew during the Korean War

Neil thought calmly about his problem, as always, and found a solution. He grabbed the correct cord, pulled it, and his parachute opened. He drifted down safely. Neil Armstrong flew seventy-eight missions in the war and received five medals for his bravery.

But Neil's most dangerous challenge was yet to come. After the war, he joined NASA to work in aeronautics. He became an astronaut in 1962. Four years later, in 1966, Neil made his first trip into space aboard the *Gemini 8* spacecraft. He stayed in orbit around the Earth for less than ten hours. When the spacecraft suddenly spun out of control, Neil calmly solved the problem and brought *Gemini 8* safely back to Earth.

In January 1969, Neil was selected to lead the Apollo 11 mission to land on the moon. When asked how he felt about becoming the first man on the moon, Neil replied, "What I really want to be, in all honesty, is the first man back from the moon." On July 16, 1969, the Apollo 11 mission launched. Three days later, Neil and his fellow astronauts Edwin "Buzz" Aldrin and Michael Collins were orbiting the moon. Neil and Buzz then got into the *Eagle*, the tiny spacecraft that would land them on the moon.

The Eagle

As the *Eagle* neared the moon, Neil looked out the window. Dozens of large rocks covered the landing site! Neil steered the *Eagle* away from the dangerous rocks. But the *Eagle* was running out of fuel. Neil flew the *Eagle* carefully, searching for a safe place to land. Finally, Neil gently landed the *Eagle* on the moon. There was only twenty seconds of fuel left!

Neil's footprint on the moon

"The *Eagle* has landed," Neil Armstrong told the world. He was able to communicate by radio and TV. For the first time in history, people were on the moon. Neil put on his special space suit. He slowly climbed down the *Eagle*'s ladder. Back on Earth, millions of people watched. Then Neil Armstrong stepped into history. He put his left foot down onto the moon!

"That's one small step for man, one giant leap for mankind," Neil said. Neil took a few more steps, leaving the first human footprints on the moon. And because the moon has no wind or rain, Neil Armstrong's footprints will remain there for many years. Once a young boy who had only dreamed about flying, Neil Armstrong had flown to the moon.

Roop, Peter, and Connie Roop. *Take A Giant Leap, Neil Armstrong!* New York: Scholastic, 2005.
Wagener, Leon. *One Giant Leap: Neil Armstrong's Stellar American Journey.* New York: Forge Books, 2004.

ANIMAL RESEARCHER AND SCIENTIST

Jane Goodall
1934–present

"You have to be patient if you want to learn about animals."

— **Jane Goodall**

Jane Goodall trudged through the African rain forest. She climbed steep hills. Insects bit her. Her light brown clothes clung to her damp skin. Jane heard rustling plants, cracking sticks, and strange hooting noises. She glimpsed furry animals disappearing into the forest. Jane knew that a group of wild chimpanzees was nearby, but she could not get close to them. Would she ever be able to study the chimpanzees she had traveled thousands of miles to see?

Eventually, Jane did get to see the chimpanzees. She watched mother chimps kiss and care for their babies. She saw father chimps find food and groom one another. She smiled as young chimps wrestled and played. Jane was learning things about wild chimpanzees that no one had ever known before. But how did Jane come to dedicate her life to chimpanzees?

Jane was born on April 3, 1934, in London, England. From an early age, Jane loved animals and was curious about them. When she was one and a half years old, her parents gave her a stuffed toy chimpanzee named Jubilee. Jane carried Jubilee everywhere. Today, Jane and Jubilee have been together for nearly seventy-five years!

Mother chimp caring for her baby chimp

One day, when she was five, Jane wondered how chickens lay eggs. She followed a chicken into the henhouse to find out, but she scared the chicken away. So Jane decided to hide in the henhouse until one of the hens came back. Jane didn't tell anyone where she was. She waited patiently in the hot henhouse. She didn't hear her worried family calling her. After four long hours, a hen strutted in. Jane watched as the hen laid a large egg in its straw nest.

Jane raced to share her exciting observations. Instead of scolding her disappearing daughter, Jane's mother calmly listened to Jane's story. That day, Jane learned a lesson she remembered all her life: "You have to be patient if you want to learn about animals," she later said.

When she was older, Jane formed a nature club — the Alligator Club — with her sister and two friends. When they hiked, Jane always recorded everything they saw. They collected plants, insects, and snails. Jane labeled everything, and the girls created a museum displaying all of their finds in the greenhouse in Jane's grandmother's backyard.

Jubilee, Jane's stuffed toy chimpanzee

Jane loved to read about animals and faraway places, like Africa and India. Her favorite books were *The Story of Doctor Dolittle*, *The Jungle Book*, and the Tarzan series. Jane dreamed that she would go to Africa one day.

Years later, Jane's dream came true when she traveled to Africa to visit a friend. There she met Dr. Louis Leakey, a famous scientist who was studying early humans. Dr. Leakey recognized Jane's passion for animals. He saw how determined Jane was when she made up her mind. And Jane had made up her mind to study chimpanzees!

Dr. Leakey believed that studying chimpanzees would help scientists understand the first humans. Most people thought his idea was crazy. Jane didn't. She convinced Dr. Leakey that she had the patience to study wild chimpanzees to see how they compared to early humans.

With Dr. Leakey's support, Jane and her mother traveled to the Gombe Stream Reserve by Lake Tanganyika in eastern Africa. They camped in the rain forest. Early each morning, Jane searched for chimpanzees. She found out where and what they ate. She found out where they slept. She heard them call to one another. Every so often, she glimpsed chimps high in the trees.

Slowly, Jane's patience paid off. She learned that the chimps traveled in small groups. She watched them eat fruit, nuts, seeds, and leaves. Then Jane made an exciting discovery! She saw chimps eating a baby pig. No one had ever seen wild chimps eat meat.

David Greybeard taking a banana

Jane carefully recorded chimpanzee sounds and actions. She began to know individual chimpanzees by their looks and habits. Jane named them — David Greybeard, Flo, Fifi, and Goliath.

One day, David Greybeard came to Jane's camp. He ate nuts from a tree in the camp. He took a banana the cook had saved for Jane's dinner. Within a month, David Greybeard was taking bananas out of Jane's hand! David Greybeard also approached Jane when she was in the forest. When the other chimps saw that Jane was not dangerous, they let her get closer. The chimpanzees began to trust her.

David Greybeard opened another important window into chimpanzee life. One day, he stripped leaves off a long stem and poked the stem into a termite mound. Then he carefully pulled out the stem and ate the termites covering it. David Greybeard had made a tool! Before Jane saw this happen, scientists believed that only humans made tools.

Jane's discoveries about chimpanzees have excited people around the world. Her work has inspired more scientists to patiently observe animals in the wild. Jane has studied chimpanzees for almost fifty years now. She has written books and articles about them. She still travels the world helping chimpanzees, which are now classified as "endangered."

David Greybeard eating termites from the tool he made

Jane helped found Gombe National Park where she first did her chimp research. She created the Jane Goodall Institute, which supports chimpanzee research, reforestation efforts, and zoos for orphaned chimpanzees. Her Roots & Shoots groups encourage young people to learn more about animals, to work to protect them, and to preserve their habitats.

Jane has dedicated her life to chimpanzees. Through patient observation and hard work, she has expanded our understanding of chimpanzees. In turn, the chimpanzees have changed and enriched Jane's life. Jane wrote, "I hope you will be inspired, as I was, to do all you can to make the world a better place for all living things."

Goodall, Jane. *The Chimpanzees I Love: Saving Their World and Ours.* New York: Scholastic, 2001.
Goodall, Jane. *My Life with the Chimpanzees: The Fascinating Story of One of the World's Most Celebrated Naturalists,* rev. ed. New York: Aladdin, 1996.

AFRICAN AMERICAN WORLD WAR II PILOTS

Tuskegee Airmen

1941–1946

"Every time we climbed into a plane, we were carrying the weight of the entire black race on our backs."
— Lt. Col. Lee Andrew Archer, Jr., a Tuskegee Airman

On March 7, 1942, five young men stood at attention on the one runway at Tuskegee Army Air Field. It was a day they had dreamed about for years. It was a day that many other African Americans had dreamed about, too.

The **Tuskegee Airmen** were a group of 992 African American fighter pilots, plus their air and ground crews, who served heroically in World War II. These first five men were the foundation of this group. Their names were Benjamin Davis, Jr.; Charles Debow, Jr.; Lemuel Custis; George Roberts; and Mac Ross.

But these men and many others had to fight for the right to fight America's enemies. Their battle began in World War I, when Eugene Bullard became the only African American to fly in that war. He flew for the French Air Force, fighting against the Germans.

Runway at Tuskegee Army Air Field

In 1922, the courageous Bessie Coleman learned to fly in France, too. When she returned, Bessie became the first licensed African American pilot in the United States. Other African Americans wanted to fly as well. Some took private flying lessons and became pilots. Others created flying schools for African Americans. Some joined flying clubs. But their numbers were small. In 1939, when World War II broke out in Europe, there were only 125 licensed African American pilots in the United States.

African Americans were not allowed to serve as military pilots. Still, many wanted to join the military. Some joined the army. Others joined the navy. But, as in the rest of the country, these soldiers and sailors were often segregated from their white colleagues. They ate in separate mess halls, slept in separate barracks, used separate showers, and served in separate units.

These brave men were willing to fight for freedoms in faraway lands that they frequently did not have in their own country. Charles Francis, a Tuskegee Airman, wrote that African American pilots had to "fight for the right to fight."

African American leaders pressed the government to enlist more African Americans into the military. Finally, in December 1940, the United States Army Air Corps, which later became the United States Army Air Forces, made plans for an experiment: African American pilots and ground crews would be trained for their own separate unit.

The government decided to train these men at the famous Tuskegee Institute in Alabama. This college had been started by Booker T. Washington and had educated hundreds of African Americans. The pilots would attend classes at the institute and practice flying at a nearby airfield.

The Tuskegee Airmen Bronze Medal

Thirteen men were inducted in March and began training in July 1941. The men studied hard in and out of class. They learned how to fly. They practiced takeoffs and landings. They practiced spins, loops, rolls, and sharp turns. Each new pilot knew that one day he would be facing enemy pilots and would have to use his skills to survive.

The training was so hard that only five men completed the courses and got their "wings" — not many, but it was a start.

More men followed the first five "Tuskegee Airmen," until there were enough pilots to form the 99th Fighter Squadron. By the end of the war, 992 pilots had earned the right to be Tuskegee Airmen.

In 1943, the 99th flew its first mission. From a base in Africa, the 99th attacked Pantelleria, an Italian enemy island. The 99th destroyed trucks carrying ammunition and blew up storage depots. They escorted bombers who blew up other targets. They even shot down two enemy planes.

Island of
Pantelleria, Italy

African American pilots of the 99th became so good at protecting bombers on their missions that they were nicknamed the Red-Tail Angels, for the red tails on their airplanes. In one day, they shot down five German planes. Two Tuskegee Airmen, only firing their guns, sank a German ship.

But as good as the pilots of the 99th were, they also had losses. Enemies shot down planes. Planes accidentally crashed. Still, the 99th fought on. They flew more attack missions over Italy. They escorted more bombers. Back home, newspapers carried stories of these heroic African American pilots. One Tuskegee

Airman said, "Every time we climbed into a plane, we were carrying the weight of the entire black race on our backs."

While the Tuskegee Airmen were fighting the Germans in Europe, other African Americans were fighting segregation in America. When sixty African American officers tried to enter a "White-Only" officers' club, they were arrested. This incident, and the protests that inspired it, pushed the military to integrate its bases.

Red-tailed airplane

The Tuskegee Airmen flew their last combat mission on April 30, 1945. The war against Germany ended eight days later. The Tuskegee Airmen had flown over sixteen thousand missions and attacks. They had destroyed hundreds of enemy airplanes, tanks, factories, trains, and boats. And they had won more than nine hundred military medals and awards.

But the Tuskegee Airmen also won something more. They won the right to fight as Americans with equal rights. Their heroic efforts changed the air force, and helped change the country.

Since that day in 1942 when the first five Tuskegee Airmen received their pilots' wings, many other African Americans have flown in combat as pilots. Since 1983, twenty-three African American astronauts have been trained to fly in space. The experiment at Tuskegee was a success for all Americans.

Francis, Charles. *Tuskegee Airmen: The Men Who Changed a Nation*. Wellesley, MA: Branden Books, 2002.
McKissack, Patricia, and Fredrick McKissack. *Red-Tail Angels: The Story of the Tuskegee Airmen of World War II*. New York: Walker, 1995.

Muhammad Ali

1942–present

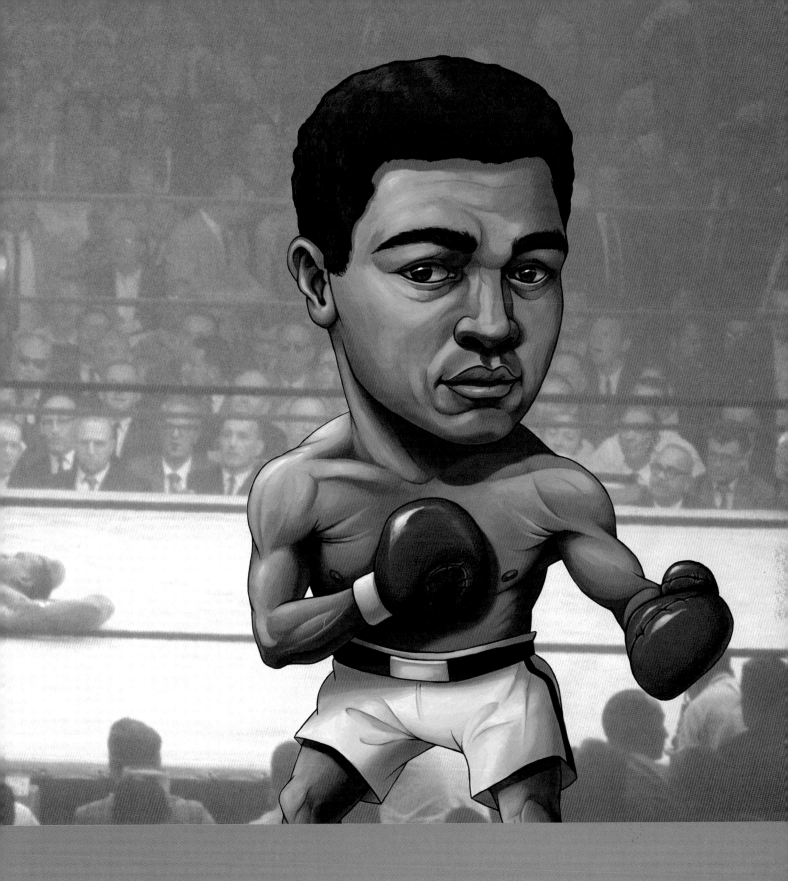

"Float like a butterfly, sting like a bee!" — **Muhammad Ali**

Cassius Clay was born in Louisville, Kentucky, on January 17, 1942. One day, Cassius Clay would change his name to Muhammad Ali. With this name, he would go down in history as the world's greatest heavyweight boxing champion as well as a champion of peace.

Cassius grew up in a loving family. He and his younger brother, Rudy, were close friends. Sometimes, when they were playing, Cassius challenged Rudy to hit him with a rock. Rudy never hit him because Cassius "was running left, and right, ducking, dodging, and jumping out of the way." Later, as a boxer, Cassius used these same skills to defeat his opponents.

Ali's red and white bike

When he was twelve years old, Cassius became a boxer because of a fight that never happened. That day, Cassius rode his red and white bike to a fair. While Cassius enjoyed the fair, someone stole his bike. Cassius reported his stolen bike to Joe Martin, a police officer. Cassius told Mr. Martin he was going to "whup whoever stole my bike."

In his spare time, Mr. Martin taught young boys how to box. Mr. Martin told Cassius, "Well, you better learn how to fight before you start challenging people that you're gonna whup."

Cassius trained seriously. He worked hard learning how to box. He ran in heavy boots to strengthen his legs and build up his lungs. He didn't smoke or drink. Later, Cassius said, "I was the first one in the gym, and the last to leave."

Soon Cassius was boxing on *Tomorrow's Champions*, a local
television show. Cassius ducked, dodged, danced, and punched
as he fought. His method was to "float like a butterfly, sting
like a bee!"

Cassius joined the U.S. Olympic boxing team. He won a gold
medal in Rome in 1960. He proudly wore the medal day and night.
Cassius came home to a warm welcome. The mayor of Louisville
told Cassius that his gold medal was the "key to the city."

But Cassius was soon reminded that, even though he was
an Olympic champion, he was also an African American in a
segregated city. Like Rosa Parks; Martin Luther King, Jr.; and
millions of other African Americans, Cassius could not eat in
restaurants with white people. He could not play in "White-Only"
parks. He had to ride in the back of the bus.

Cassius had experienced
discrimination before, but now
he felt he should be treated
better because he had
won a gold medal for his
nation. Cassius was so
disgusted that he threw
his precious gold medal
into the Ohio River.

Cassius realized that
he had to do something to
make life better for all African
Americans. He decided to become
the best boxer in the world and to use
his fame to help others. Cassius said,

*Ali's Olympic gold
medal floating in
the Ohio River*

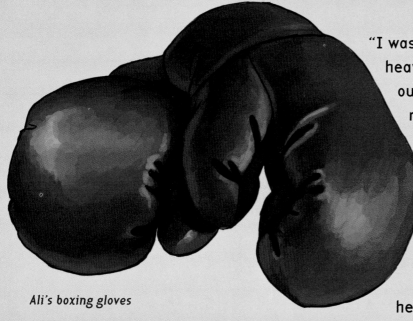

Ali's boxing gloves

"I was fighting to win the world heavyweight title so I could go out in the streets and speak my mind. . . . My plan was to dance, stay out of my opponent's reach, and use my wits as much as my fists."

And he did. In 1964, Cassius Clay beat Sonny Liston and became the world heavyweight champion. Two days later, Cassius Clay changed his name to Muhammad Ali. "Muhammad means 'worthy of all praises,' and Ali means 'most high,'" Ali explained. Cassius had joined the Islamic faith and did not want his old name anymore. Ali said, "Changing my name was one of the most important things that happened to me in my life."

In 1967, Ali's life changed again. The United States was at war in Vietnam. Ali believed that the war was wrong. His religion told him not to kill people. Ali refused to join the army. "We become heroes when we stand up for what we believe in," he explained.

Ali went to court to fight against the government's order to join the army. He battled for four years and won this fight, too. But Ali's decision to stand up for his rights cost him his world heavyweight title. The World Boxing Association refused to recognize Ali as champion after he took his stand. Ali would have to fight to become world champion again. In 1974, Ali fought George Foreman in what was called the Rumble in the Jungle. The fight was staged in Africa. Ali won and was world champion again.

In 1978, Ali was beaten by Leon Spinks. Ali was no longer the world champion. But he was still the "People's Champion," fighting for equal rights. Ali challenged Spinks to another fight. This time, using his wits as well as his fists, Ali won. He was world champion for the third time. No heavyweight boxer had ever been world champion three times!

When Ali retired from boxing, he used his many talents to help others. He worked with children with disabilities. He traveled the world encouraging people to fight for their rights. He served as a United Nations Messenger of Peace. He met with world leaders. He gave speeches. Ali was honored for being both a boxing champion and a people's champion. He was given the Presidential Medal of Freedom and was named one of the top athletes of the twentieth century.

But then Ali got Parkinson's disease, an opponent he could fight but could not defeat. His arms shook. He could not talk very well. But he kept his sense of humor, his honor, his determination, and the twinkle in his eye.

Ali returned to the Olympics in 1996. This time, he lit the flame at the opening ceremonies in Atlanta, Georgia. Ali also received another honor in Atlanta. He was given a new Olympic gold medal to replace the one he had won in 1960.

Today, Ali works to help others through his charities and his Muhammad Ali Center in Louisville, Kentucky. He has traveled the world, but he never did learn who stole his bike that day when he was twelve and started him on his heroic journey.

The Olympic torch Ali carried at the opening ceremonies in 1996

Ali, Muhammad. *The Soul of a Butterfly: Reflections on Life's Journey.* New York: Simon & Schuster, 2004.
Myers, Walter Dean. *The Greatest: Muhammad Ali.* New York: Scholastic, 2001.
Smith, Charles. *Twelve Rounds to Glory: The Story of Muhammad Ali.* Cambridge, MA: Candlewick Press, 2007.

TENNIS PIONEER AND CHAMPION

Billie Jean King
1943–present

"I want to play tennis forever." — **Billie Jean King**

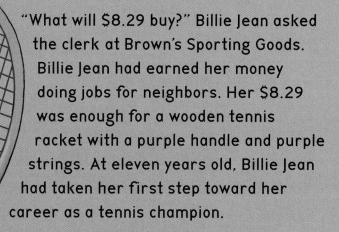

"What will $8.29 buy?" Billie Jean asked the clerk at Brown's Sporting Goods. Billie Jean had earned her money doing jobs for neighbors. Her $8.29 was enough for a wooden tennis racket with a purple handle and purple strings. At eleven years old, Billie Jean had taken her first step toward her career as a tennis champion.

Billie Jean Moffitt was

born on November 22, 1943, in California. Billie Jean was a superior athlete. Taught by her athletically gifted father, Billie Jean learned to throw and hit. She learned to race, jump, dive, and slide to catch balls. By age ten, she could throw a softball faster and harder than many high school girls could. At this young age, Billie Jean helped her softball team win an all-city championship.

Billie Jean played football, too. In her neighborhood, she excelled as a placekicker and a running back. She also played basketball, but she was asked to quit the elementary school team. She was too good! Because she was tall and strong, no other students could get rebounds or score against her.

Billie Jean's life changed in fifth grade, when she met her friend Susan Williams. Susan asked Billie Jean if she played tennis. Billie Jean did not know how tennis was played. Susan explained that tennis players jump, run, and hit balls. Billie Jean loved jumping, running, and hitting balls. Her first chance to lob a tennis ball over a net was with Susan, at Susan's family's country club. Billie Jean soon discovered that the local recreation department offered free tennis lessons. Her instructor, Clyde Walker, made

Billie Jean's first tennis racket

a game out of the practice drills. Billie Jean had fun as she learned to hold the racket, hit the ball, and run for a shot. When her mother picked Billie Jean up from her first lesson, Billie Jean said, "I want to play tennis forever."

Clyde Walker immediately recognized Billie Jean as a talented athlete. Clyde gave dedicated and determined Billie Jean extra lessons. On weekends, Billie Jean played tennis from nine o'clock in the morning until it was too dark to play. She competed in her first tournament after only nine months of playing. She defeated her first opponent, but lost to her second.

Billie Jean focused all her energy on tennis. She read about tennis. She watched tennis on television. She practiced ground strokes in the living room, occasionally knocking over lamps. She practiced her backhand and forehand strokes against a wooden fence in her family's backyard. The fence was no match for Billie Jean's strong strokes, so her dad replaced the battered wooden fence with cement blocks. At night, Billie Jean slept with her tennis racket. She dreamed of being the best tennis player in the world. She dreamed of winning at Wimbledon's Centre Court.

Wooden fence Billie Jean practiced against in her backyard

Wimbledon has hosted international tennis tournaments since 1877. Winning a championship on Centre Court, on Wimbledon's lush green grass tennis courts, is an essential step toward being ranked the number-one tennis player in the world.

It was difficult for Billie Jean to get the money she needed to compete in tennis tournaments. Despite this obstacle, by age sixteen, Billie Jean was ranked the fourth-best female tennis player in the United States. At age seventeen, she missed her high school graduation to compete at Wimbledon. Billie Jean and her tennis partner, Karen Hantze, won doubles at Wimbledon, the youngest pair to win this honor. This was just the first of twenty championships that Billie Jean would win at Wimbledon.

Wimbledon trophy

In college, Billie Jean met her future husband, Larry King. They became engaged just before Billie Jean left college to play tennis full-time. Billie Jean needed to play tennis all year to move from number-two to number-one tennis player. Her coach, Mervyn Rose, helped Billie improve her serve, grip, and forehand shot. Off court, he required Billie Jean to study other tennis players' techniques. Billie Jean's physical and mental tennis game became a match for the best in the world.

Billie Jean married Larry King in 1965. One day, her friend Muhammad Ali leaned over and whispered into her ear, "Billie Jean King, you're the Queen."

Billie Jean King was the queen of tennis. She worked hard to carve out her professional career and to make the path easier for all female athletes who followed in her footsteps. When Billie Jean rose to the top, women were not treated as equals in the athletic world.

In 1973, Billie Jean served an ace to the world when she beat a man, Bobby Riggs, while millions watched. By founding the Women's Tennis Association, she helped female athletes receive an equal slice of professional sports prize money. She used her fame to help pass Title IX, a law

Mrs. King Wins Battle
Mrs. King Defeats Riggs 6-4, 6-3, 6-3 Amid a Circus Atmosphere

Newspaper headline when Billie Jean defeated Bobby Riggs

that helps girls have equal access to sports. Billie Jean continued to share her tennis skills by coaching other players, including the 2000 U.S. Olympic team.

"Each generation stands on the shoulders of the pioneers who came before," Billie Jean explained. Today, tennis and sports equality stand on the shoulders of this female tennis pioneer.

Lannin, Joanne. *Billie Jean King: Tennis Trailblazer*. Minneapolis: Lerner, 1999.
King, Billie Jean. *Pressure Is a Privilege: Lessons I've Learned from Life and the Battle of the Sexes*. With Christine Brennan. New York: LifeTime Media, 2008.

FIRST HISPANIC SUPREME COURT JUSTICE

Sonia Sotomayor
1954–present

"I do believe that every person has an equal opportunity to be a good and wise judge, regardless of their background or life experiences." — **Sonia Sotomayor**

Sonia Sotomayor was born on June 25, 1954, in New York City. Each of her parents had moved to the United States from Puerto Rico during World War II. Sonia's father had a third-grade education and worked in a factory. Before she met Sonia's father, Sonia's mother had served in the Women's Army Corps. In New York, she worked as a telephone operator.

Sonia grew up in the Bronxdale Houses, a public housing project. When Sonia was eight years old, she learned she had diabetes. A year later, Sonia's father died. Sonia was very sad, but she was always comforted by her mother and her brother, Juan.

Bronxdale Houses

Sonia's father had spoken only Spanish. Her mother spoke both Spanish and English. Sonia spoke Spanish and began to speak English only after her father died.

Sonia's mother had to raise Juan and Sonia by herself. She held a full-time job, but she also went to college at night to become a nurse. Education was very important to Sonia's mother.

Sonia said, "For my mother, as a single parent, education was paramount. We did without a lot of other things, clothing in particular." But the Sotomayors were the only family in their neighborhood to own a set of the *Encyclopaedia Britannica*.

Encyclopaedia Britannica

Sonia loved baseball. She grew up near Yankee Stadium in the Bronx and has been a dedicated Yankees fan all her life. Sonia said, "You can't grow up in the South Bronx without knowing about baseball." She also enjoyed reading. Some of her favorite books were about Nancy Drew, the girl detective. Sonia dreamed that one day she too might be a detective.

But it was Perry Mason, a lawyer on a television series, who inspired Sonia to pursue a career in law. Sonia said, "I watched how every time Perry wanted to do something, he had to ask the judge for permission. . . . I realized that the judge was the most important player in that room."

Sonia worked very hard in school. In high school, she was recognized as the most outstanding student in her class. In 1972, Sonia went to Princeton University in Princeton, New Jersey, on a full scholarship. She majored in history, which gave her a

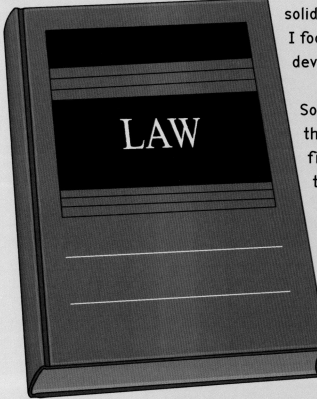

Law casebook

solid background for working in law. "Once I focused on becoming a lawyer, I never deviated from that goal," Sonia said.

Sonia graduated from Princeton in 1976 with the highest honors possible. She was the first Latina to win the M. Taylor Pyne Prize, the top academic award at Princeton. Sonia began law school at Yale University in New Haven, Connecticut, that same year.

Sonia focused her energy on learning all she could. She studied hard and edited the *Yale Law Journal*. Stephen Carter, one of Sonia's friends at Yale, said, "She was always in the library, always had a casebook under her arm." He also said that Sonia "always had a manner that was open. She didn't put down other people."

After graduating from Yale in 1979, Sonia practiced law in New York City. She tried many cases and learned even more about the law. In 1991, President George H. W. Bush nominated Sonia to serve as a U.S. district judge in an important New York court.

While serving on this court, Sonia helped end a strike in Major League Baseball — a strike that had lasted 232 days and had led to over 900 games being cancelled, including the 1994 World Series. Many sports fans felt that Sonia had "saved baseball."

In 1997, President William J. Clinton nominated Sonia to serve on the U.S. Court of Appeals in New York City. On this court,

Sonia helped make many more legal decisions. Because of her knowledge of the law and her strong work ethic, one of her fellow judges said, "It is both a pleasure and an honor to serve with her."

But Sonia's work was not all in the courts. She worked in her community to help disadvantaged youth. She encouraged judges to bring their daughters and other young women to court on Take Your Daughter to Work Day. She mentored young students. She even held a pretend trial for Goldilocks to teach these students about courtroom rules.

In 2005, *Latino Leaders Magazine* named Sonia one of the "101 most influential individuals in the [U.S.] Latino community." Three years later, *Esquire* magazine named her one of the "75 most influential people of the 21st century."

But Sonia's biggest honor came when President Barack Obama nominated her to serve on the United States Supreme Court. When asked about her ability to serve on this court, Sonia said, "I do believe that every person has an equal opportunity to be a good and wise judge, regardless of their background or life experiences."

On August 8, 2009, Sonia was sworn in as an associate justice of the United States Supreme Court. She became the first Hispanic Supreme Court justice, and only the third woman to serve on the highest court of the United States.

Baseball bat and ball

American Bar Association. "National Hispanic Heritage Month 2000: Profile—Week 4, Sonia Sotomayor." American Bar Association. http://www.abanet.org/publiced/hispanic_s.html.
Biography Reference Bank. "Sonia Sotomayor." *Current Biography*, October 2009. H. W. Wilson. http://www.hwwilson.com/Currentbio/cover_bios/cover_bio_10_09.htm.
Office of the Press Secretary. "Judge Sonia Sotomayor." The White House. http://www.whitehouse.gov/the_press_office/Background-on-Judge-Sonia-Sotomayor/.
Stolberg, Sheryl Gay. "Sotomayor, a Trailblazer and a Dreamer." *New York Times*, May 26, 2009. http://www.nytimes.com/2009/05/27/us/politics/27websotomayor.html.

★ FIRST AFRICAN AMERICAN PRESIDENT
OF THE UNITED STATES

Barack Obama

1961–present

"My heart is filled with love for this country." — **Barack Obama**

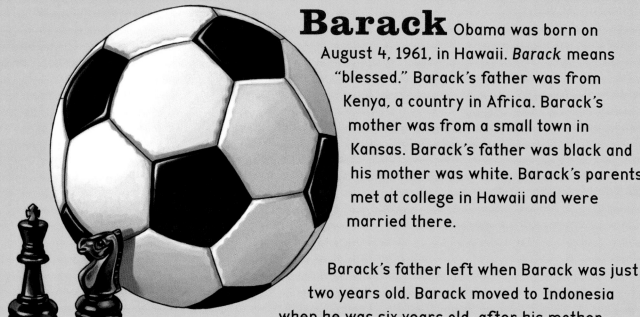

Barack Obama was born on August 4, 1961, in Hawaii. *Barack* means "blessed." Barack's father was from Kenya, a country in Africa. Barack's mother was from a small town in Kansas. Barack's father was black and his mother was white. Barack's parents met at college in Hawaii and were married there.

Chess and soccer— two of the games Barack's stepfather taught him

Barack's father left when Barack was just two years old. Barack moved to Indonesia when he was six years old, after his mother married Lolo Soetoro, an Indonesian. Lolo taught Barack how to play badminton, chess, and soccer.

Living in Indonesia fascinated Barack. He made new friends, he learned to speak Indonesian, and he saw many unusual sights. Barack even had a small ape and two crocodiles living in his backyard!

Barack's mother knew that a good education would be the key to Barack's life. She woke Barack at four o'clock in the morning on school days. Barack studied for three hours before he went to school.

When Barack was ten years old, he returned to Hawaii. There, he saw his father for the last time, when his father came for a Christmas visit. In Hawaii, Barack lived with his grandparents while he went to the Punahou School. Throughout his years there, his grades were good, he read many books, he wrote for the school magazine, and he played on the basketball team. His nickname on the basketball court was Barry O'Bomber. Even today, as president, Barack finds time to play basketball.

Barack graduated from Punahou in 1979 and went to college in California. After two years, he transferred to Columbia University in New York City. Soon after

Barack studied very hard

he graduated from Columbia in 1983, he worked as a financial writer, but he knew he wanted something more in a job than just the chance to earn money.

So Barack moved to Chicago. He worked with churches and other groups to find ways to improve people's housing conditions. He worked to make schools better. He worked to clean the streets and get better garbage pickup. He worked to clean parks and playgrounds.

After three years, however, Barack realized that he could do more if he became a lawyer. Then he could make sure laws were better enforced and people got the help they needed more quickly.

Before Barack went to law school, he visited Africa to meet his relatives who lived there. Although Barack's mother was white and his father was black, Barack has always thought of himself as an African American. His father had died in a car accident, but Barack met other members of his African family. He also visited his father's grave. Barack felt as though he was getting to know his father for the first time. He realized that his father had been filled with hope for the future. Barack came home filled with that same hope for a better future.

Barack went to Harvard Law School in 1988. He studied hard. In 1990, Barack was so well respected by his fellow students that he was elected president of the *Harvard Law Review*. The *Law Review* is a special journal written by Harvard law students. Never before had an African American been elected president of the *Harvard Law Review*.

After law school, Barack wrote *Dreams from My Father*, a book about his own life. He returned to Chicago to teach, practice law, and help register Illinois voters. Barack had met Michelle Robinson after his first year of law school. They were married in 1992. The Obamas have two daughters — Malia, who was born in 1998, and Sasha, who was born in 2001.

In 1996, Barack was elected to the Illinois state senate. He helped make laws to improve people's lives in Illinois. In 2000, he decided to run for the United States House of Representatives. In Congress, Barack could make laws to help all Americans. He campaigned hard, but lost.

But Barack did not give up. In 2004, he was elected to the United States Senate to represent Illinois. He was only the fifth African American ever to serve in the Senate.

Barack's Harvard graduation cap and gown

As a senator in Washington, D.C., Barack often went to the Lincoln Memorial to think about his life and the role he wanted to play in America. He thought about Abraham Lincoln and Dr. Martin Luther King, Jr., and how they had helped to change America.

Barack wrote, "My heart is filled with love for this country." Through his speeches and his books, Barack's popularity grew. People began to recognize his name across the country.

The Presidential seal

In 2007, Barack decided to run for president of the United States. Barack announced his decision from the steps of the Illinois state capitol building in Springfield, Illinois, the same town where Abraham Lincoln began his journey to the presidency.

Barack knew it would be a long, hard campaign to convince Americans to vote for him. He went from state to state meeting people and giving speeches. More and more people supported Barack. Finally, on November 4, 2008, Barack was elected the forty-fourth president of the United States. He became the first African American to hold this position.

That night, President-elect Barack Obama said, "If there is anyone out there who still doubts that America is a place where all things are possible . . . tonight is your answer."

Dougherty, Steve. *Hopes and Dreams: The Story of Barack Obama.* New York: Black Dog & Leventhal, 2009.
Obama, Barack. *Dreams from My Father: A Story of Race and Inheritance.* New York: Crown, 2004.